Hotel Eliseo

by Harry Eyres

Hearing Eye

Published by Hearing Eye
99 Torriano Avenue,
London
NW5 2RX

COPYRIGHT © HARRY EYRES 2001

ISBN: 1 870841 824

This publication has been made possible with the
financial assistance of London Arts.

Printed by Catford Print Centre
Typeset by Daniel James at mondo designo

To all the people who have helped me through

Contents

I

II

I

Snow Photos

In photographs the world is bright,
snow freshly fallen on the cedar,
white the garden; father is smiling

woolly hat on, coffee mug
in one hand, holding in the other
the broad-bottomed Aga kettle;

and see! past those humps of cars
the bare bones of a beech
almost dissolved in sunlight.

But all these scenes are framed:
I may look pretty, says the cedar,
but my branches will not bear the weight,

and father, through his smiling,
wants to clear the path,
defrost the iced-up Austin.

Growing Up *(in memory of Ethel Espin)*

The year the mark on the door
showed me taller than you
I felt like a giant.

You were tiny, round and grey;
we thought you were imperishable.

The kitchen was your kingdom;
you ruled with a rolling-pin
and stern retorts: "Ifit" (for "if it comes");
"shimshams for meddlers" (when we asked for more).

The dough was mercilessly pummelled,
dug deep with firm, arthritic hands,
kneaded into shape and left to rise;

the pastry slapped down on the flour-dusted table,
rolled, and trimmed around the edges,
rolled again.

I watched from table height,
rising, little by little,
in the warm.

Dough *(in memory of Ethel Espin)*

It all went into the mustardy yellow bowl,
the speckled flour, warm milk, hot water, gruesome
treacle—and what have I forgotten?

I am becoming dough. I feel
the warm liquids sinking in,
absorbing my dry dustiness,
my milled and sifted lightness,
absorbing me completely.

I have fibres. I adhere.
I am pulled upwards, and outwards,
in all directions.
I am pummelled and gathered
and stretched,

taking in air,
taking on life.

I forgot the yeast,
a sour-smelling crumble
bought by the quarter-pound
in a creased paper bag which I blew up and popped;

the unpalatable secret which made the whole thing rise.

Fireflies

I think I'm seeing stars—
little points of greenish light;
the field is full of fireflies.

We go out after supper and try to catch them.
You sit on the cut grass in the dusk full of noises.

I am beside you; I am watching you watching and listening;
I think: I could put my hand out and touch
the source of all light and life.
My hand trembles at my side.

Later we catch one, without thinking;
a black glossy thing,
it dies out on us.

The Long Freeze

A year now since the long freeze started.
The smooth-skinned beech-limbs are bare
in the narrow copse; underfoot the leaves are very dead.

We have had snow: white windless days
numbing the withered nettles, killing the nerves
in brittle stems, suspending the movement of the moist air

in an exhalation…

Ghosts

This is the memory-house,
dark, Gothic, rather forbidding
with the tall pines outside
and the tiny chapel.

(In fact those gables are Elizabethan.)
You can't get into the upstairs rooms;
they're crammed with jumble,
jumble upon jumble.

There's a leak in the roof:
father is up there on a ladder
but he won't make it any better.

One day we unbricked
the old chimney in the kitchen:
the bricks were thicker than we thought
and when we pickaxed through
there were tons of rubble smoking.

The ceiling in the drawing-room
with the long Tudor fireplace
is getting lower all the time;
less light comes in at the lattices.

In the end we had to sell up.
The place was bought by a City slicker
who laid down gravel for his Daimler.

But sometimes in the far garden
there are parties lit by lanterns
hung from branches;
tall stories of a great tent pitched,
the remains of fires,
hurdy-gurdy music winding back the centuries,
the former folk in fancy dress
drinking wine from paper cups
and falling out of trees.

Mr Appleby

I am digging for you, old man, gardener,
turning over the clods of memory
to unearth your crusted tubers.

Trousers: there's something to hold on to,
as thick and black as the old coal sacks
you slung over your shoulder
with a nonchalant ease at seventy.
And your tarry, earthy smell...

To see your face, the peaked cap you always wore,
I'd need to crane my neck;
but no-one could forget your bushing thick white hair,
the clearness of your gap-toothed smile.

We had discussions about flowers;
it was the vegetables I rooted for.
You let me take down to the kitchen fistfuls
of young carrots tender as minnows,
shaking the black earth from round the
curly fern-fronds of their new green ears,
and crunch their sweetness with my milk-teeth.

The same colour as the carrots was
the robin who perched upon your
momentarily rested spade and eyed us
for worms.

The garden where you worked's grassed over now.
A row or two of raspberries scratch on
where all your summer cornucopia
ripened: strawberries, sweet peas,
spiky artichokes, the heaped-up beds where the secret
asparagus lay half-buried then sprang
like young tipped sex; black-eyed broad beans
and wrinkled cabbages.

You lived to ninety-seven, lucid, smiling,
a widower for quarter of a century. In the end
the years dragged when you couldn't manage
walking up that steep hill to the pub. Now
all the digging's left for me to do.

The Winter Fields

I stepped out in the winter fields;
I could feel the light going through me
and through and through.

Lots of details disappeared.
They went into the maw of time.

There was a tearing and a shredding;
parts of me were being rubbished.

I would never be accommodated
in my native fields and farms.

The Kiss

Yes, in that very chair
turned at a slight angle to the window
(I have not moved it since)
you were sitting then

when, standing by you
and feeling powerless
to move nearer or farther,
but that it was now or never,
daring and not daring,
after our hands touched, then clasped,
I finally kissed you

and as the light drained slowly out
(it is doing so again now)
we continued kissing, sometimes
sitting, sometimes standing,
or half-leaning against the cushions on the sofa,
taking our fill and not our fill of one another
until the last drop of light was gone.

Writing Poetry is So Easy

Writing poetry is so easy
and costs virtually nothing!

All you need is paper and pen
and yourself, in a certain frame of mind,

able to drop down a bucket
into the well of deep being;

sometimes the rope isn't long enough—
you go on releasing it into the dark,

letting out more and more
without a splash or a ripple

and you think, it's gone dry,
I've dried up, or

there is water but
this rope will never reach it;

you can't see down there,
it's all black,
it could swallow you!

Or again
you might strike water
and when you haul it up
it smells bad:

a bird or a rat or a dog
or even a human being
died down there:

maybe that human being was you.

Writing poetry is so easy
and costs virtually nothing!

Hotel Eliseo

Like others of my age at various times
I've done the Italian tourist thing—
the luminous sky of Venice
twice so far in a lifetime
to be grateful for.

When I wasn't looking at Carpaccios
or making annotations in the Accademia
about (I think) Titian's late Pietà

I was having hot thoughts about tarts
in a smelly pensione
while grappling with Henry James's *Golden Bowl*
and getting tangled up in the same paragraph night after night;

or musing autumnally about history and my failure to score
among the dun reeds near the duomo of Torcello;

and then on the long train back to London
can remember clearly the unshaven
Romanian and his pretty, shy girlfriend
five days travelling without food
taken pity on by the kind Italians
and the Swiss who kept me up all night
repeating that he couldn't sleep on trains.

Florence of course: a dusk vigil
on the top floor balcony
of the Pensione Sorelle Bandini
drinking fiascos of Frescobaldi's Chianti
admiring the cypresses over towards Fiesole
and wondering if she might, or whether
he was gay, or both really preferred
art (I mean the thing that painters do).

And Rome: two unexpected meetings
with the green-eyed beauty I mooned after
in my first term at university:
her admission that if it had just been a question
of her personal life she would have killed herself
and that one week of an affair
had felt good, desiring and being desired.

But nothing compares with the very first time:
the thrill of flying clean over the gleaming Alps,
being told this was St Peter's dome,
the artichoke hearts at the Trattoria Piccolo Mondo
which my mother loved;
phoning up for breakfasts in bed, the whole family
for once all in it together,
the sumptuous lift of the Hotel Eliseo.

Tips for the Traveller

Travel light; leave in the morning;
resist the temptation to become familiar;
stick the bags in the boot and hit the road.

Your reward will be clear windy mornings,
eagles overhead (almost within reach!),
distant views of the sea and mountains.

Leave no trace of yourself behind
except some sand maybe,
a used ticket in the ash-tray.

Bajo de Guía, Sanlúcar de Barrameda

That shore across the estuary looks so inviting,
the sun glowing in the pine trees,
that ruined, abandoned house,
the white birds wheeling.

Here everything is concrete and litter:
signs telling you to stop, go, wait, or not wait;
people loitering who may want to talk to you;
nondescript buildings petering out into the distance.

You could pay a fisherman to ferry you across;
it would take ten minutes;
you could step on the sand of that other shore;
maybe from there this mess would make more sense.

There you would find the glow
mysteriously faded from the pine trees;
that ruin, close up, is a barracks;
the birds have moved off into the wood.

Being in Love

Autumn? It had never happened to me before.
Coming back in the train from Gatwick
the incandescent trees held me transfixed—
I was still in a daze when we got to Victoria
and left my bag with all the stuff from Spain
on the rack above my seat; ran back; found it again
untouched…

        I was seeing the world in a different
light
still weeks later, composing love letters
and playing Chopin's B major nocturne
with too much feeling for the notes to gel.

Your redolent responses followed; dried flowers;
Catalan poetry girlishly inscribed
in a thick Italic nib; elegiac
comments about our time together
in the mountains, which had "changed your mood,
made life worth living again,"
though not with me.

        Months later,
mooning about in freezing January
I photographed you in high heels in the snow,
slightly out of focus.

Invitation, towards evening

Take this path with me,
the garden on one side—
birds roosting towards evening—
past the white wall,
the steps down to the sand.

The headland stretches out
a long dark arm to sunset;
the sibilant waves bear messages,
relaying them repeatedly, if only you would listen.

Come closer, into that warm trail of light;
throw off everything you no longer need;
strike out your own way.
The sand is firmer here and darker,
the current not as treacherous as you think.

Bolonia, January 1992

Whale Burial

Flaccid, beyond recognition,
your soft remains are littered on the beach.

Flung up on this coast between continents
a week ago, you had form and substance.

People came to inspect
your unearthly proportions.

Once a generation such a marvel happens;
you give names to places.

You began to dry and rot
simultaneously.

You sagged and aged,
a ship-sized bag of bones and juices.

Downwind it smelled like a fish factory,
but you retained vestiges of yourself.

Now your dissolution has gone too far:
it has become a public nuisance.

A small army of men, the burial party,
a grave as big as a house.

The earth-scooper scrabbles ineffectually,
trying to grasp your slippery secretions.

It spreads you out further and deeper.

Parts of you seep into the sand,
membranous sacs of blood and semen.

Your skeleton is distributed
among the people.

Your jaws will be rejoined as an arch
through which air and pilgrims pass.

Your penis will be hung up in a bar,
 a lewd and leathery baton.

No reliquary can hold your bones,
but still I am thinking of that beach,

and those men, too many for the job,
staring, with their hands in their pockets,

at an enormity.

The Real Thing

We leave the city for a town.
We leave the town for a village.
We leave the village and walk
down a track
past a ruined mill.

This is the real thing at last—
Romantic poetry!—
lovers under the mountain moon.

In a complicated manoeuvre
I undo your bra and pull it out
through the sleeve of your sweater.

Big Bang

A gun goes off in the night.
The guilt-stricken miller
who murdered his mother
took a pot-shot at the moon
which kept spying on him,
which knew he had done it.

Your breasts are full moons
with mountains rising, firming,
aureoles like dark craters round them.

Your mouth is a black hole
which sucks the whole world into it
with innumerable stars and plancton.

My mouth is a black hole too
luckily: we balance the universe between us;
we swallow each other; we don't swallow each other.

All time ripples out
from that first explosion.

Clean Sheets

There are seams in these sheets
where there shouldn't be.

You wake up cramped by creased lines,
sagging into a bed of peat,
your limbs hunched towards
postures of birth and death,
assuming ancestral deformities.

You are not getting any younger or straighter.

You dream of the clean sheet of that beach
stretched wide and taut as canvas
primed by high tide:
the words alighting
to justify the margin
like sanderling which hug the water's edge,
so light, so skittering fresh.

Erasable, renewed,
the spiky script they leave behind.

Perfect Poem

Washed up on the beach
ages and ages ago

I had timbers and entrails;
I wanted to live.

I panted and cried out,
I felt I could be saved.

But no-one rescued me.

They wouldn't come close
(the smell must have been terrible).

My innards were turning,
turning like fish-guts in a bad wind,

or pickled into a paste,
a delicacy for far-off emperors.

So I was bones, spars,
odd knots of rope,

strict economy of signs
denoting shipwreck.

The wind went on refining me,
the sand rubbed at my edges,

polished me so smooth
I became like pebbles,
like sand itself.

The salt cured me,
and cured what was already cured,

until there was only salt
and the wind

and the faint fine smell
which is no longer I
but the sea,

and now the people come from everywhere
and lie on me and bathe in me.

Unwritten Poem

This is a poem
I'm not going to write,

or a poem
left as a draft
in a notebook

like the letter
where you say what you really mean

which you can never send
or finish, even.

"She was here"

"She was here, she left
hardly any time ago...

The door is open, you can
step inside—"

The intimate air still breathes
her shallow breaths;

the floor is her bare soles,
warm, grained, smooth;

the furred tick of the clock
is her pulse, her secret heart.

Keep quiet, you might wake
the hollow pillow,
the abandoned, tangled sheets.

Leave now, leave those things
slowly, over days, weeks, months
to exhale her absence,
in their long dark sleep
shake off those deep impressions
and resume their proper shapes.

Father

This habit of checking before speech
I've noted as characteristic:

a stuttered, not quite uttered
word of praise, encouragement,
love even;

the hang of the head, set of the jaw
tell their story:

enormous pressure against
what's almost said.

The Tears of Things

We all have to die and the world is rich in onions—
globed roots with tough brown skins which guard
their pearled and peeled whiteness. The onion cries
when you slice it crosswise; it sheds a liquid
like the shine on eyes, the tears of things. This
crystallises on the crunchy rings which mark
a growing outwards. Here is in its way
a perfect living form. It makes you weep.

Maps' Happiness

Maps make you happy!
Cradled in their safe grid
the ways are plain
to the ends of the earth.

Beautiful irregularities
of coastlines! Broad bulge
billowing out from
the narrow suck of the Wash!

Sky-scattershot of archipelagoes!
Up there the Hebrides
prance like sea-horses—
platter of fabulous crustaceans!

All their inlets have been
noted, yet retain their privacy;
the roads go only so far;
then a margin of space and the sea.

The Vulture Speaks

I can see you down there
but you don't interest me.
You have no taste
yet.

The Wreck at Littleferry

You failed in your mission
of being useful.

Once a buoyant vessel
bridging the gap,

sooner or later
you hit rock bottom.

It all fell away from you,
coverings, contents,

leaving a bleached rib-cage
pitched up among pebbles—

or only half a rib-cage.

But what is there
is unmissably there:

timbers framed
to strong design,

foot-long nails
rusting for decades,

hinges that will outlast
generations of molluscs

though not the lichen
which has taken hold

nor the rip-tide, the terns,
angel-arrows, plunging.

Fried Fish

You have the look of disillusioned visionaries,
your great round unclosable eyes,
your pursed lips, your clenched and jutting jaws.
The horizon must have seemed infinite,
a remote white pearling or clouding;
but you saw no horizon, just the element
stretching for ever in front and around
mixed with eddies, bubbles, breath of other fish.

Now you lie stretched in a row on my plate
well salted as if by a subtle, final insult,
soon to enter the sputtering, unutterable martyrdom
of boiling oil, in which your open black eyes
will cloud over, go pearl and pop out.

Golden Oriole Ballad

(inspired by the voice of Bob Dylan)

I walked through a wood,
didn't meet anyone at all,

following a voice, a call—
some inhuman fluting

which kept me walking;
it moved ahead of me constantly,

a wood-spirit hopping from tree to tree
belonging to nothing I could clearly see;

from clump to clump among the oaks it went
and I clambered over boulders and sweat

wet my neck for the heat
was beginning though it was morning still.

I stopped at a spring and took my fill
of cool water running clean from that hill.

Then it came again, that call beyond words
and not of this world, it carried so far

and sounded clear
and stood out above the sounds that were near:

would I never catch up with it
never even see the singer of it

who was leading me on,
name what I couldn't yet envision?

I stopped in the track, I was
near despair, halfway to no place,

for the goal kept moving and no recognition
was given that I could count on.

Was I chasing a phantom,
some beautiful delusion

not worth getting lost for
down that path right out of my road?

I was thinking that thought with my head in my hands
when I met a man, a native of those lands

and I asked him about that obsession of mine,
what was it calling so clear and so fine?

The old man replied, 'That's the oriole's song,
the golden oriole', and he smiled as he went his way along.

And the darkness of my mind just started to clear
because I had a name now for what I could hear;

even if I could never get close
that bird, I was sure, I would never lose.

II

Some Days

Some days I don't seem able to write or speak;

days when everything's held
blankly on trust
in a white light that's like darkness:
every dead leaf and brick
and live blade of grass
the same shade
and the sky neither clear
nor cloudy;
neither sun nor rain nor wind
waiting

for the black and white spotted woodpecker
to grace the small bent tree beneath my window

with its strange, rapid attentions,
its bright scarlet crown.

Visitors

I don't have a view on the street.
My friend the successful journalist
has a view on the street, where the action is.
I look over back gardens
which repel attempts at gardening,
at corrugated iron sheds
and sepulchral white doors
and skeletons of prams
stranded on extension roofs.
I look at the last yellow leaves
of the pollarded chestnut
hang, swing, droop and drift
all the way down the stunted trunk.

I may say however
that distinguished visitors
pay me calls: the kestrel
on the rake of the TV aerial
two gardens down can preen and ruffle
and shake and shift its weight,
test the grasp and snap of its claws;
the piratical jay with a blue feather on its shoulder
makes the cherry-branches shiver
in a scatter of wrens;
and the a capella choir of goldfinches—
my Quattrocento angels—
floats in to feast on thistle-seed;
and in among the pile of dog-eared bricks
nest door, the vixen raised
a family of cubs, playing out
their youth for all it was worth
one early summer, May, June,
then July they were gone.

Photograph with Clouds, Sun and Rain

In that part of the picture it's raining;
here the sun is shining.

It's raining here
but look, over there, a valley in the sun.

A worn-out track; cactuses;
a thorny tree; let's take the path

together and see
what we shall see.

I'm sitting in a ruined fort
reading a novel

with a sad ending; sitting quite happily
watching a landscape of clouds

and sun, warm sun,
and rain, rain which the parched land needs.

Oaxaca, July 1992

Gerald Brenan at Yegen

You put a thousand miles,
two thousand books,
between you and a deaf father, the War,
the fags and philistines of school.

You landed in a village up a mountain,
a people absorbed in their own doings,
uninterested in "where you came from",
who accepted you and did not moralise.

You could not have asked for more;
distance was what you needed:
looking across the valley towards the sea and
Africa
you drank great gulps of the unending air

and freedom. Time opened up
before you and all round,
the snow-fields at your back, larks singing,
your long life's work all ready to begin.

'A door opens'

A door opens
        the sun steps in:
angle on a summer garden,
        young beech leaves
faun-dappling
        a shadowed lawn;
hibiscus sticking out
        its rude red tongue at morning.

I shut the door
        in front of me—
too much paradise—
        and run upstairs
to my books…

'But of course'

But of course
        nothing is stable:
not ourselves
        not what is not ourselves.

Under the taut
        sea surface
like satin stretched
        over a woman's skin
which is smooth as satin

the tectonic plates
        rub
heave
        shift
the continents
        ourselves.

Midsummer Evening

Last night the sky caught fire—
a red glow, a red burn,
and I hoped something terrible had happened:
at last the great wished-for conflagration.

I was watching TV at the time but no-one
interrupted the programme;
it was the same games, the old films
unravelling:

midsummer evening after a day of leaden skies,
the obstinately slow dying out of the blaze.

'Else a great Prince'

What's this, what's this?
On a day like today, so warm
you're shuffling about in beach shoes
and outside the chestnuts toss
above the roofs in the wind and great heat
and you're making salade nicoise in the kitchen,
all work finished for the summer,
what more could you want?

But still something cries out, 'I'm trapped'
—you stop with the fridge door open—'free me:
"else a great Prince in prison lies."'

Easy to dismiss such voices, like those
which tell you, on no account leave the house
today, or step on the cracks in the pavement, you will die.
Don't do this and that, the fearful voices say.

But this one's different, a voice before words,
a shudder and a shiver through the bones
seeking its release in breath.

You can carry on as before
doing what must after all be done;
or stop and listen, with the ice-box melting,
catching the drips, writing the unfrozen tears down.

A Green Dream

I warned you but you would go
under the green water near the hollows
by the mill race. I watched you
swim green as that water, feel your way

out of my sight.
                   I held my breath—
I was counting the minutes, pacing the bank
and nothing, except after some while
a string of bubbles from the unclear depths
which died as their round mouths kissed air.

I had known it all along. Then I saw you
lying dimly on the bottom. Then I dived
to embrace your sodden body, hauled you ashore,
gave you, gave us the kiss of life.

You moved in throes.
A whole young world of tears
gushed out from mouth, eyes, nose and ears.
From your chest the breath leapt. On your face
the angry brows, expression of bewilderment.

Our Berlin Together

Thank God I'm not in Berlin this autumn!
This is not the Tiergarten, it's Regent's Park
and the leaves are late turning this autumn
and squirrels are still promenading in the park
and I even feel sympathy for the bow-legged,
leery, sideways-hopping crows.

A heap of discarded clothes behind the goal
of a teenage football game is close to their owners:
in the air which is mild and blue hang gulls.

A year ago it was Berlin and much colder.
The Tiergarten was a forest with few ways through
and down by the Wannsee we plodded along
the streets of grey half-shuttered villas
and men in uniform were herding up the leaves
into great colourful mounds, like heaps of
discarded clothes, like mounds of old shoes.

I hate Germany, you shouted after a row with a bus-driver
who wouldn't stop because we weren't standing at precisely the right spot;
and I felt embarrassed and wanted to dissociate myself from you
but the fact was I hated Germany too,
our Germany together. I woke up stiff in the mornings,
in all the wrong places. Your despair was growing.
Breakfast at the Hotel Bogota could've been jolly but wasn't;
the room-rates had gone up since our friend stayed there;
they were eating up your dole money; you accused me
of trying to cheat you; it was a complete disaster.
The Ku'damm's parade of styleless luxe repelled you:
no way was this the town of Sally Bowles.

On the last day—too late—we discovered the East.
Streets of heavy apartments had survived the War;
new bars were opening everywhere.
In Potsdam Sans-Souci was ringed by Soviet blocks
but in the Afghan Organic Cafe some gentle people
at last laughed softly together.
There was hope now if we'd cared to stay.

November 1995

and now the world breathes out
and turns upon its axis
and draws the colour out of everything
and turns its face away slowly;

and I reach over to the other side of the bed
half-expecting to find your scented side,
your soft freckled moon-shoulder
to rest my palm on.

Speaking Things, Brixton

A little girl's shiny black shoes
sitting on a window ledge neatly together
(they've been there several days now);
the girl with the cap worn sideways
hardly breaking step as she looks in through the window
and sees me writing in the cafe;
a young man's eyes staring intently at his lover,
as rainclouds form over the railway arches
with the clumps of buddleia pushing up, their roots
in mortar;

          a notice attached to a lamp-post
saying my favourite cat, the one who used
to sidle up and demand to be stroked
has been run over, but not killed
and is now in the animal hospital.

The Limit of Vision

Two people are walking along a path by a river
in the evening, in the shortening light.
The river runs smoothly on towards the sea,
the path follows it. As the light is fading,
the couple don't know how near the river is to the sea,
how far off the bulky mountain is,
looming to the north. A pair of swans
has settled on the far bank
near the limit of vision. Now one
of the couple stumbles; they decide
to turn back. Everything is quite serene
and they will never know how close they came
to where the tame thickets of the path
open on the uncluttered margins of the sea.

Beauly River, October 1995

The Song of the Cranes

We wait for the wind to change,
picking at last autumn's
spoiled corn-husks.

When nature seems most dead
we know our moment, spiralling upwards
on huge wings.

We fly all night; our cries
are moon-trumpets, star-muted, long-
dawn-drawn-out,

until we reach our stamping-ground,
tread incandescent lakes and
mate for life.

Migrating south, we post up
letters in the sky, signifying
everything.

The Spinners of Dreams
(after Las Hilanderas by Velázquez)

This is where the dream-work happens,
in the healing dark: soft arms, delicate fingers
card and twist and spin and weave;
the leavings litter the clayey floor.

Two steps up the fine people are framed—
Gods, heroines in a glittering tapestry:
one of the ladies in her silks looks down
with pity on the lowly spinning girls.

Oh my lovely spinners carry on the work
with your rolled sleeves, your dimpled arms,
your bare feet braced against the earthen floor,
pull me, stretch me and unravel me

here on this lower level in the dark,
here where crude stuff is woven into dreams.

Chameleon

When I failed to fit in
the world turned on me.

I retreated into camouflage.

But however perfect the disguise
you can't *be* your surroundings.

There's a distinction to be made,
a stone, unblinking eye
and a cruel, projectile tongue

which bides its time
then hits the exact spot
of your obliviousness.

Leavings

You left your woman things behind—
creams, hair-gel, box of tampons, a few t-shirts.
Once before you threatened to make a clean sweep
of all those replaceable or irreplaceable objects,
then relented,
bequeathing me these relics on the shelf.

Stuck above the fireplace, the photo
of us two with a full moon in May
halfway up a South Down
has keeled over, curled over itself,
folded:

Do you want me to fold?
you used to ask, in bed,
so you nestled your head
on my left shoulder
with my left arm curled round you,
folded itself,
and enfolding then.

Saying Melon

The way you said melon came
into my mind this morning
as I went to the market
to buy a melon. What came
into my mind first was the
thought of buying a melon,
then your voice saying melon.
You put on a funny voice
when you said melon. You became
a two-year-old who couldn't quite
manage m's and l's,
whose lips and tongue hadn't yet
hardened into the final
division of consonants.

Missing Each Other

"Do you miss me?" you asked
on the phone
when I'd gone on some solo trip
and come back late
to an empty room.

Or "are you missing me?"
(see how quickly tenses blur).

"Did you miss me?" when we got back
together after a time apart.

How could I answer your questions?
I didn't know what missing meant.

Now I can say "I miss you.
You missed me.
We missed each other."

Tryst

So we sit in the smoochy "Anchor" bar
and you give me your life story.

This was why you lured me here
to this late-night tête-à-tête

to tell me about the times of depression
how for the first twelve years of your marriage
you hated sex

then fell in love with a handsome journalist
but when it came to the crunch wouldn't consummate

the affair. I sit there nodding my head, offering
therapeutic comments. I know my place.

I'm biding my time, waiting for my turn
in the Ancient Mariner's chair.

To My Friend Who Runs the Jacaranda Café in Brixton

Are we enemies, you and I?
Class enemies, race enemies?
Once I heard you say: "The English
were worse than the Boers, at least
with the Boers you knew where you were.
The English hid it all under
the mask of politeness."

You're very polite, too.
We greet each other guardedly,
sometimes a smile breaks through.
What are we hiding, each of us,
beneath the mask of politeness?

Not Quite

We sat opposite each other on the wall
beside the river, quite near the church.

We sat opposite each other, not touching,
not quite touching, not yet.

There was something between us, something
we didn't quite know how to reach.

It was almost spring. The swans thought so.
The sun was shining (quite bright).

The sun was shining and the young leaves
were not quite yet out.

It was quite warm. It was not quite evening
in the not quite (almost) spring

and the words in the space between us
on the point of speaking what we couldn't, quite.

After June Thunder

I'm sitting by this pond on a grey
not warm June English afternoon;

grey willows are reflected in the olive-grey
water and the grey clouds hold the key.

Grey is not uniform, grey can lighten or darken
or just dissolve away, blow into thin shreds;

but something here holds the grey in place—
both a promise and a withholding:

with grey we know where we are, we can bed down
in grey, which doesn't dazzle but coolly cushions,

which allows the fine distinctions of flowers
and burns nothing off but maintains the borders.

We can spend whole days, whole lives in grey, with the
heat
never quite coming through, the garden protected.

Distant thunder rumbles but there's no electric
storm or cathartic downpour; we're still forever

held in whatever it was we thought we might
one day come out from under.

The Colour of Love

Oh mother, I've been thinking harsh thoughts
about you. Through therapy I've become more aware
how you lived your life through my achievements,
how you closed the gap between us and stunted me.
Now I look at these sprouts, these purple sprouts
with their slender stems and little leaves
like ears coming off the stems and the
purple colour they leave in the cooking water.
You grew this vegetable in our garden,
you introduced me (at a tender age)
to purple-sprouting broccoli which
softens like my heart in the boiling water
with the rich stain of sadness seeping out
through the pierced colander and down the drain.

Harvest

In high summer it's midwinter.
Oh heavy heart, you don't recognise the seasons,
you should be set fair, warm and dry,
a comfort on my left side to lie on.

All you can do is shudder, endlessly
bringing up the clouds, the tears—
and these are only the beginning, you tell me.

This year's harvest will be another sodden one.

Tea-rooms, Stratford-upon-Avon, November

A girl arrives bringing candles,
thick, white, ecclesiastical candles
on black, cast-iron tripods:
the black legs root into the table-cloths,
the tall stems reach up to the light.
How much I long for candle-light,
not this overall glare without shadow,
for the mercy of tender, intimate light,
for the nakedness of the living flame,
erect and wavering against the shadow
as the day darkens and the year darkens
and November yields up its ghosts.

Roadworks on the Westway

For years the advertised improvements
only seemed to slow you down.
"Expect delays until the next millennium,"
"we're thinking of you and your needs."

Now after all the grind of lane closures,
use of the hard shoulder, contraflow,
diversions taking you at right angles
to where you thought you wanted to go

you suddenly see it has actually got better.
You no longer need to go backwards to go forwards.
The way is freer and faster and the time is shorter.

Remembering Omagh (for Paula)

i

We stopped off in Omagh
on our way west to Yeats country

finding (pure chance) the Serendipity Café—
you had a scone, I had a chocolate eclair.

It was peaceful there. Two women were chatting
and puffing thick smoke. A little girl said,

"Don't smoke, it's bad for you", and we smiled
and the women went on smoking

and two big square-shouldered men
sat at another table and talked about cars and the racing.

ii

Driving through your country
I find my own flag

flying at farm gateways
still defending the prime land

from the bog-dwellers,
the old cut-throat chieftains.